feria: a poempark

feria: a poempark

Oana Avasilichioaei

WOLSAK
&WYNN

Cover art and design: Anthony Burnham
Author photo: Terence Byrnes
Typeset in Goudy
Printed in Canada by The Coach House Printing Company

Wolsak and Wynn Publishers Ltd
69 Hughson Street North, Suite 102
Hamilton, Ontario L8R 1G5

The publishers gratefully acknowledge the support of the Canada Council for the Arts, the Ontario Arts Council, and the Book Publishing Industry Development Program (BPIDIP) for their financial assistance.

Library and Archives Canada Cataloguing in Publication

Avasilichioaei, Oana
   feria : a poempark / Oana Avasilichioaei.

ISBN 978-1-894987-29-5

   1. Hastings Park (Vancouver, B.C.)--Poetry. I. Title.
PS8551.V38F47 2008   C811'.6   C2008-903721-9

origin is unoriginal
not a beginning
                    simply a point
in space crossed
        and recrossed with stories

Prologue

In the poempark   the seasons spill
as one.
Each line: a tree planted
grows roots; the roots tunnel beneath the page.
Limbs stem.

Occasionally, a small shudder
is a thought misremembered.

The poempark is domestic.
Words carefully placed and arranged assemble.
A wilderness.

At night, the howl of beasts   imagined
keeps us awake.

The poempark has no river running through it
for at times the poempark is itself
a river.

The architect considers the poempark. In the mind's eye
this lasts seconds   or a century.
Then, in a sudden furious burst   always unexpected
the architect draws the poem. A schema
of geese, word-drops and birches. Into a park.
Writes the park. Into a poem.

Branch, footpath and stanza model its nature.

A void bordered.

Some days, visitors
flood the gates in hoards.   Enticed.

Then for months   the park, exposed to the elements, waits.

                                        Neglected.
A barely tangible breeze stirs the grass
reminds the park   that it is indeed.

some streams

Origins or The Book of Questions

Is risking an act of

spring, the sunrise between sleep
a lily

      breaking?

                     The book is thick.
                     If filled with words
                     will it be thicker?

If a question mark didn't

the possibility of a question
its existence
its wolfishness

In this book there are no keys.

*

A slaughterhouse built in haste. A new city demands meat.
A city will have its meat.

A slaughterhouse built
because it can't be helped.

1869	Land Auction, New Westminster
Lot #26	purchased
George Black	buyer
The Slaughterhouse	a shack

boarded with rough lumber, hand-split cedar roof

He casts his lot
twenty five down, twenty five later
not exactly game
but a land of hemlock
and swamp, cedar and scrub.

1863

The land, lacking
pioneers, has to be   divided
                             and numbered.

A piece of forest
with a small stream   lot number 26.

                             A meaningless equation
                             perfectly understood
                             in pioneer language.

This is not a riddle.
A place you go to find laughter. Thick,
abundant. Laughter you can hold
in your hands. Laughter   you can laugh at.

This, a slaughterhouse
built over a stream.
The stream blushing into Burrard Inlet.

*

In the building of a book
there are techniques
one must learn
to keep wolves out.

Early morning   have the blinds drawn in the east
                     and open in the west.

Afternoon reverses.

Though the windows stay shut
all day long.

*

George Black, a worldly man, doesn't begin
with cattle and meat
but with a seaside resort.   1865

                              Down the stream,
                              (later the red stream, later pushed
underground to make way
for horse racing and roller coasters)   ocean-side,
                              Brighton Hotel is built.

A hotel and a slaughterhouse. And a stream in between.
Black new to this wilderness. This coast. And him not looking back.

Of course, as usual in these sort of circumstances,
the smell is a problem.
Also the cattle skulls, the bones.

*

Is the slaughterhouse a confession?
The fire pit out back a mouth left open?
The pulley and hook the ghost of a word? The word of a ghost.

*

A word can travel back in time, invent its origin, its muse.

Hastings Mills, Hastings Street, Hastings Park, Hastings
Hotel, Hastings Townsite, Rear Admiral George Fowler
Hastings, Khanamoot.

*

When he dies
Black relinquishes a few heirlooms: a plank road
                              a burned hotel
                              and a widow.

The widow has nightmares.
At night
she strolls the Scottish countryside
mouth filled
with sweet scent of broom.
But when she wakes
                    Oh sorrow!
                    This cursed coast!
Nothing   but moss
                young mountains
                and eight months of rain.

Water   diligent
works on the soil   loosens
                          and the soil drains.

Surely the ocean ever encroaching
tide always coming
never going
> Where is that spit of sand
> she swears she saw
> ten years back.
> And the forest
> once looming
> now dead logs hug the shore.

The widow panics.
She digs out old storybooks

reads instructions about the Ark
and sells the five acre lot
to the BC Gas and Electrical Company
for one hundred and fifty thousand dollars.
The same day, she books a train to Halifax
and a cabin on the first ship
back to paradise.

*

Inwards stories are foreign
render the skin puckered
pulley and hook
                a park with no history
the book opens and questions
leaves imprints
        in the wet grass
    in a room of floorboards and old sweat
hooks a pulley into a muse

cattle hung by an open mouth
and blood draining 1865 1863 26

road planked over the old Musqueam trail back to Khanamoot

*

How to invent this man?   The slaughterhouse fire pit
What shudders at the root of a story? now merely an idea.
What shudders at the root of him?   Long filled in, closed up, built over
Need? Before language.   a child's ferris wheel
                                 an army barrack

a red, red barn.

In the red barn, the cement floor gives way in places
                    to uneven lumps
                    floor slightly raised.

Beneath – a resting place for cattle bones, stories petrified.

This is George Black's legacy.

Each year the bones work themselves
closer to the surface, threaten
                    to break through.

The caretaker (mute by childhood) signs to park officials.
Something must be done.

*

Ancestry   a footpath in the park
barely visible   torn loose
                              wolf driven.

Along the path a long list of firsts settled: the first
          the first   the first
At the closing of a century
each first obsesses a first
civilizing a land into the worshipped other.

What was lost?   What was found?

no dreams to speak of

Where language was languages. In things
grown   things cared about.
Words are meagre these days
hungered
words wake into wakefulness reluctantly.

*

If to slip into the hole of the park

In this cell hope to flourish.
In this cell hope becomes
to speak a passion. Limbs'
humid petals, pages risking
open.

Below the window a day sits waiting.
Later, cattle will stroll with the day, cattle shoulders
remembering the buzzing of flies.
But now she is

in a childhood bookcase
a magic-book.

Museum

when
a column
of smoke
is a column
steam   is   confused

when when is an artefact
when is

if a boy   a figure
if a park   dreams
                  we receive a dowry
                  green

a merry-go-round
                      built   1912
                      we read quickly, confident

                      though   misled
              1917   says another

if a puzzle
          wasn't so utterly trustworthy

then we were   vacuous
we let language wander as if she could have her pick of many suitors

                  mindful   stay calm
                  mindful   of those 36
                          wooden horses carved by prisoners' hands
          stay

when was it built exactly?

1904   says a third

if a merry-go-round could   remember

I am twirling   restored, removed, canopied,
pink-cherubed, mirrored, filigreed   I am twirling
though at the centre
                        still

Spirit of the West!

"Never   spirit of the west,
brook no obstacle   the Hastings Park
                    carven   heart of   forest
wilderness,   critical   citizen
and visitor is   exhibition and playground,   nature
eminent   fitted   the most   kind   west…

            a short while ago   nothing   densest
woods defy   the hand of man   change   the primeval
            now   manufacturers   east   west   north
      south   display   their wares
commodious   livestock   all   on exhibition
crowds of throbbing humanity pour   along the
'skid road', the future   removed from the first
condition of things."

Vancouver Daily News – Advertiser, August 16, 1910.

"   it   pervades
    man, woman and child
                whether   cultural
    commercial,   or sublime.
      let the people
doorstep   slowly
    elope   a people's gigantic   ground
worthy of a progressive   , a progressive   a
progressive   ."

J. J. Miller in Vancouver Exhibition Association. *Bulletin* No.3, 1912.

"   since the outbreak   we
exhibit   A false   possession of
                                                      war
                              the Imperial and Dominion

                                                                    inspiring
          people to

                                        communities   of
danger and unrest."

V.E.A. *Bulletin* No.9, 1918.

"   fine arts,
horticulture, women's work,   cattle, sheep and swine
            cage birds,   ,   ,   , minerals
school
            the Exhibition.
depart   the great   number   exhibits come
        .   citizen   is hobbies,   interests,   business.
                                            the other fellow
            anxious   where he stands,
                            held   separate
                    so
shown

                                    held.

industrial exhibitor   can be summed up in a   few words
        :   space
                                    space

space
space every year   from the very first, we think
we say all that is necessary."

V.E.A., Replies to Resolutions and Questions Submitted by the Civic Committee to the Vancouver Exhibition Association. (excerpts), 1925.

"   to have   Indians here is to
show   development

                      [of Indian Affairs]   …. to
         display   reservations
                                 evidences   the

industry of   Indians."

J.K. Matheson to Dr. Duncan Scott, December 13, 1927.

"The whole   of ancient
                              day   is
                                        horse   , cow
        , sheep, pig , rabbit   goat   dust !   lets

                              kick   partition
        terribly   stay
                        now...
                                                a thin lump
straw   ,   , an   army blankets

        ...   blankets
                every
                age   –   a pathetic
privacy...   cry   , say
                              to such a place... there are ten
        how   for 1,500   ."

Muriel Fujiwara Kitagawa to Wesley Kitagawa, April 20, 1942.

"   culture in all its phases   will
be   major imp   ,
            the Board of Control   at   attention
                        of our provincial   act
            henceforth lumbering
                        tourist   must be vigorous
aggressive   sore   and   red."

"We   record   being whole   the
Department [of   fence]   war   for   want
                 will interfere with   the
Department   no   use
buildings, we shall   return   ."

Minutes of the Executive Committee, V.E.A., November 15, 1944.

"We   fair   so. We
          great family of fairs
     dominion   the border."

"The Pacific   seemed to be wearing the
     curious,   sombre   mother
          stand
          time   possess   her material
     ."

Minutes of Annual General Meeting, PNE, December 12, 1957.
Minutes of the Board of Directors, PNE, September 19, 1962.

"Too often   a burden
                                  traffic
                 development
        mammoth invasion
                 I know that that can't be washed away,
                          the PNE
                    community.

                                                                    We
   lost   .
   We lost
                                                           ..."

Hon. Mr. Williams (NDP), February 22, 1973.

The "Gayway"

feria   rips   open
   lies exposed
           the park's red heart
   beating on the muddy earth

Through this door, ladies and gents,
the petrified woman awaits.
Are you a doctor sir? A scientist perhaps?
Step this way and see the wonders of the universe.

feria   loses itself
   crowds
familiar among strangers

Come one, come all, and marvel
at Independence, our educated horse.
That's right, a human brain! She will amuse you,
amaze you. Just drop your nickel in the box.

feria   isn't light
                    as fairies
        pale, fair, nor impartial
        this word won't talk to birds

        They'll whirl and sway, give you a wink
        or two. Our Orientals and Salome Dancers, Spanish Carmens
        & genuine Dutch comedians. Leave your kids
        at the merry-go-rounds. Come to the Great Burlesque!

meaning fair-game
feria   vulnerable
        is secreted

        Straight from the ancient land of spices
        and dark beauties, from the river Ganges
        to the New World, the Sacred Crocodile sacrificed
        200 years ago, now on display for your viewing pleasure.

feria   lonesome
        needs spectators
    storms inhabit this word

Cherry (1)

Childhood has gypsy fairs
not recollected in tranquillity
but hardly recollected.
to try dizzying   to have been almost as closed
                                    and final as a book.
Childhood is gypsy fairs
squatting on barren land   trampled

swings twirling like the gypsy women's skirts
multicoloured balls, whistles, string
red and green popcorn, pink cotton candy
fake pipes, plastic bracelets, rings
and dark faces   so many dark faces

childhood is fairs
gypsying

Grandmother crossing the canal
hating gypsies
                     crossing the canal
to buy a bunch of cherries, stems tied
with string.

Immigrant

Inside *The Immigrants* a girl

ashen-chested,   eyes stone-dust

        just now the world fell
        off the edge of the ocean

islanded in this park
                she is baroque
                a pearl
                imperfectly shaped

a girl who lost her tongue

        just now she flew
        off the edge of the ocean

classed into *The Immigrants*
        father, suitcase on his granite shoulder
        mother, one hand in his, the other protecting
                her daughter's back

one family arriving
            anxious   road-weary
                    signed S. Commachio, 2000

Cherry (2)

Did I not tell you mother?
The cherry tree forgot
to blossom; branches quickened   but didn't sprout.

As a statue, Columbus doesn't look anxious
he doesn't look
though his eyes are open and he holds a book.

Distraction is a cherry pit
stuck in the throat.
Shame deepens, radiant.

If Columbus was an actor
the new world a play
would you say his was a great or failed performance?
would you ask for an encore?

First, the possibilities:
The coast could wreck a ship;
a valley tilt, shudder, settle back
some gaps and flattened houses in the aftermath;
a whole forest rebel
refuse to disappear in the echo of an axe.
But then, what really happens then?
Mother, you brought me here.
Of course, he was first, we could blame him
if blame we must.

"The Genoese navigator, in 1492 after a courageous
voyage of 72 days, discovered the unknown lands of the new world."
Carved in gold lettering into the stone pillar
on which he sits. He
"The Dreamer Christopher Columbus"

How many Christopher Columbus statues litter the world?

Here, he's just a boy
sitting on a pillar
the kind you might find on a quay
with an iron ring hanging where boats tie up.
He is supposed to be possibility.

Mother, was it possible for you?

In the villages

Feet numb, nude in the surf,
sigh a garden.

In its pools, a reflection
of sky, one seagull and undelicate, empty shoes.

The beach town hangs laundry
from crumbled rock. Gusts dust in the eyes.
Dogs stray. Shrill of ducks.

A beacon. Grandmother's house.

A house on stilts
birdlike afloat over the imagined village.

Grandmother hidden in the thicket
gathers the thicket, fuel
in the wood stove.

Though not vast, the sea is considerate.
Sprays the face. Deserts the beach
into seafloor, deadwood, tales of serpents, drowned ships.

Grandmother boils cornmeal, fries a freshly-cut chicken
looks to the east, sees a dirty river, looks to the west
breathes faint incense from the old church.

Such a woman
enlarges in the thicket.

Sea ripples and dims. Visions, forgets, visions again.

A beacon. The house gardened
afloat over the imagined village.

Il Giardino Italiano

1

Conceive: these flat stone* slabs press
soil into its darkness.

Oblique   our eyes

Organic

Orbital   our

Conceive geometry of the newly made
: creek's sinews now a flat checkerboard.

(Why do we sit here, our cheeks pressed
to the hot stone, listening?)

---

* "… an organ slightly larger than skin, a structure
of inhuman love minus nostalgia or time."
(Lisa Robertson, *Rousseau's Boat*)

How these Roman weather gods, glorified
in stone.

How water. How sprouting mouths.

How we sit here.

How here.

To immigrate this garden. We colonize
the soil's darkness. We inconsolable
with its dark density.

(How fear.)

2

I invited the garden into my garden that was my own and no one else's.

I stood before my own garden and reviled her limbs.

I grew nauseous with my revelry.

I spat in creeks and veins.

I digested.

The hour had collapsed and I stood before my own garden with a creek for a vein and a crow for a mouth.

I wanted to realize my own garden but didn't know how.

I felt the present like a sliver aching beneath a nail.

I loved.

I thought I could lose language and think freely like an animal. I fought with my own tongue.

Then language allowed me other linguas and limbs and I was free once more.

I loved again.

For a time the sky was an opera and we all listened.

For one brief moment no boundary was at war.

For one brief moment no boundary was a boundary.

3

Project a park into gardens a project
drawn-out constructed orificing bloom.

"The meaning of becoming a historical subject."

Liatris lavender euphorbias blue irises gunnera
: an archive.

To make a sentence with instances
blooms a present into a present.

To mix my breath with your breath in this moment is.

Such space is the space a tree breathes mixing breath with you.
To exalt in a tree's exhalation, inhaling wind.
We are given such moments as gifts.

4

I took the north into my north and sat it down on a low stool.

I chided it for its southern inclinations, the loose equatorial belt, in danger of exposing the buttocks, the thighs.

The north was drunk and knew this.

I was seduced by Innovation and Progress.

I accused.

My ears and hands were shuttered so I accused falsely.

I fled.

I wanted to want the north sadness on my shoulders, though its unbearable vastness.

I'd goaded it to drunkenness and I knew this.

I realized fleeing was impossible.

With the north on my side I felt good.

I would resist the censor.

I would cry.

I fictionalized.

I grew sympathetic to a bird's calling, the symphony of
raindrops on meaty leaves. I recanted my beliefs in astronomy.

A leaf stirred my hand. To take the north into my north gave me
means.

I sat down on the low stool and listened once more.

Because endangerment is not a game, I could learn this.

Because I had endangered.

5

"Speaking and placing the speaking.
Such noise in the ditches –" that fence the garden.

How to inside*¹³this rainy climate. (How to host.)
Garden unused to such minute light, such bulky water.

Nona and Columbus stir a small pot of simplicities.

Brief parasites weather the liatris.

Hinge the garden of we on the historical
: your palm briefs my cheek
anchors we to we.

---

* "What would identify the speakers of the idiom"
(Myung Mi Kim, *Commons*)

6

I eroded into spectacle.

I eroded.

I had imprisoned the I and mirthed at its torture.

I became religious. I became cannibal and gorged.

I suffocated myself with my own grandeur.

I thinned.

I thinned some more.

I realized the privilege of a bow.

I bowed before my own privilege.

I squandered, everything, even you, even beauty, especially thought. Oh, how giddy I was squandering thought.

Outside I had tipped life on its side, materialed, and I tipping, insensate.

7

I was nuclear, thus empty.

I was dangerous in my emptiness.

How I was fear's will.

I took the soil into my soil.

I took the soil into my soil.

I saw its dark density was my own dark.

Grass sprouted into my being and I believed in being once more.
I achieved tenderness.

To originate again. Porous.

To not stop originating.

Momiji Garden

animal a leaf
in silence; know-
ledge sustains
a privilege briefly.
in a barn sweating
straw of our straw.

mother calls:
"how…"
we are fine,
we are fine.
yet the splatter
of rain on these
maples young
with life
makes us…

garden has only
a vague memory
of itself. in a
gurgling stream
fish stumble into

war.

relieved into
a block of stone
a few words
commemorate.

(   )

(no horsing around beyond this point)

on a bridge
staring at
goldfish.

                                    a man inconsolably wailing.

a bordered word nationing *them/us*.

daffodil
daffodils
a bonsai.

here is a garden of violence.

with onslaught
we enter. not
cautious, not
blind.

we eat we drink we tear we sleep
we animate into basic needs. we beast.

a path curves
the pond into
distances. foreign
into foreign-
ness doubly.

words
build
thin
walls.

to unmake
a human
takes one
word.

we sit on
a bridge
staring
at goldfish
and a bonsai
of daffodils.

to love doubly.
pollen, asylum
of bees. here
is a garden
of violence.

you and i are they and they are us who are them who are we and i
and are just pronouns.

caretaker shuffles
talks to birds
with his hands
in these walls
that surround:

heat, buzz and tire screech, errant
gunshot and horses' hooves in the gravel, whir of machines, water
in the estuary
of his hands.

no animals
just an empty
barn willingly
in september
willingly red

       tree veins the horizon

the book of morning
is a book of mourning

scribbled into its
margins: an epic

at the bottom of the pond
lives a building: culprit and hero.
there is a quest, a voyage to the
underworld, a war, and though in
the end peace is restored, herohood
is not.

rain: torren-
tial invalid.
weeks weeks
soils wet
of weeks.
musty wet
straw in-
valids the
weeks of wet.

inside the straw
the three; prime
number not divi-
sible by anything
but itself. the tear,
fragile, cascading
off the cheek into
a hand's abyss.

the three of the tear

tear multi-
plied often
with itself
tear, also a
prime number.
tear not a symbol
but a tear multi-
plying itself.

not divisible

inside the three
an animal. writing
the letter of needs
animals the animal.

easted from this
western pond, east-
ed past the stones   (symbols
we collect and are
collected into we

unresolved we breach)

talk of the three
bad stones: dead,
diseased, and pauper
stones, bares our
babble forward.

a lantern
between
us; snow
an animal
between us.

us: simply
pronouns.

to take the tear
into its very sad-
ness strolls my
attempt among
the borrowed scenery. with my eyes in your eyes i am less
vulnerable
to the elements.

(time unresolves us

artery of the palm
faces the palm's face
condensing air with breath

such desire
can create.
object itself.

ter-
restrial.

for a.b.

Close your eyes (1)

I dreamt a crow woke me
to tell me I was sleeping
it had flown over my sleep
wondered at its wakefulness

since then I mind crows
a little more
sleep with my eyes open

Close your eyes (2)

What can come from a bed?

a leaf of sleep
a dream cut in half by wakefulness
belief followed by disbelief
you
you again

When you watched me sleep what did you look like?

Haunted House

1

This is a place of sneaking.
                curtains partly opened.
                fences stumbled over.

Follow the river to the mouth
of the haunted house.

You will find
        two youngsters kissing in the dark
        a witch's laugh, years old, crackling, badly needing repair
        a winding railway track
        and beasts, plastic, glowing in the dark.

Where is the river?

The river is a ribbon of smoke rising from a pile of smouldering
stories.

The river is a work of art in the hands of a blind man.

(The river was.)

Hades acquired loneliness, then he acquired a wife
and a river to embrace her with.

2

When Orpheus followed the stream back to the land of the living
he was told not to look behind him
yet he did
        simply   too curious.

Stream, spring out of the ground,
claim antiquity in this territory that is all too new.

We wait

contemplate Orpheus
        his plans of rescue
        his simple, obstinate disobedience
        his forgetful stream.

We find the park lacking age.

Those with grand ideas
            spawning salmon, luscious ravines
force the stream to surface.

Don't live under a guarding hand, a spade.
Live only where your rippled story streams.

And if we muse on Orpheus
it is merely with a fondness for will, for disobedience.

So excavate. Go.
Excavate!

3

if Orpheus tears

if we dream the same dream

      love, I dreamt you were a castle
      then awoke and saw you were a stream

fall time mother packed crates
apples huddled in newspapers
one for each day to last through winter

mother always looking back

if a stream widens just a little
          bends just a little

if a small girl on mother's arm
in a tunnel of snow
a haunted house vanished

in winter the park widens
trees carry fewer leaves
among the paths almost no conversations circulate
         garden guarding the park

since mother raised me on apples and literature

the park orchards words

love, I dreamt you were a castle

since mother took me into foreignness
I knew foreignness
since then
I am only slightly familiar

4

There is rain, dishevelling the grass
somewhere above.
There is a gaze, citadeled, half-turned.

Our body shivered into play
we sneak in light
teenaged, thigh to thigh, giggling at the tattered
torso of a howling monster.

The river is insistent.

Leads to a love
long settled
in a hawk's mouth.

There is a fortress, there is
the one adored.

Because we can speak of love in this dark place
        we are elucidate

    figured, found in the river fabricated
out of wantonness, out
of a limb's hawk.

        Water laps softly at the foot of our disobedience.

It is now that we take the oars.

5

Orpheus, son of muse, river us through this foreignness.

Fictitious, spectres fooling in darkness, the classical
believes not in phantoms, only
in voyage.

To descend here
is to grip haunt
in its origin.

To descend is to frolic in these vanishings:
the park waits amused.

In the dark of two, a witch's laugh
in the need of myth, an entertainer
in the beast, a lyred beast:

to come out of its mouth and go back in its mouth.

A bird's giddiness in flight oars a river
trembling.

Answer to a love's first question.

One day in the life of a modern, populated fortress

1

Is morning ever whispered? Who has the throat?

I carry the park inside; it is my mouth.
And my mouth is of the fortress.

Fortress   a crumbling stillness

stricken
on the battlements building photographs.

Open the shutters!
Listen!

the town seeps in
                    loosened
                              unhinged
                          from time's iron gate
it is later and yesterday
     now and tomorrow
it is deafening
                 this battle in the throat

so at sunrise
I sit history on my knees and I seduce her.

2

Soiled at midday
we come upon
a public washhouse

deserted

into four basins water flows and drains
stone floor algaes.

We are borrowed

empty clotheslines whistle a few forgotten clothes pegs

though our steps on the stones are careless
our hands are ours.

Three basins   sheltered
but the fourth
             stares at the sky like an unclosed eye.

Above us the castle is a fitful dream.

3

We offer ourselves to stairs
ravenous streets
banquet of loose animals

a square cut into stone
windows
       chatter   clinking
       plates and cutlery
       laughter   a tower of tongues

You smile
       finger on the shutter
              as history evenings
                     into my cuffs   throat   pockets
A woman in fishnets and fur coat passes by

suddenly magnolias
your smile   holding us covenant   suddened into story

The much-used breeze longs now into now
       (humaned among the stones)
one hand in the embrace of another hand citoyennes between us.

4

Daily we covet the park

who air? who dust?

we, kings and queens
crowned with rubies and grass

      bent elbows roughened on hot stone
      palm on the small of back
      gentle caress of weeds on the bare calf

from this height the fortress gasps
its secret   our arched view: the o of an old bullring

      (camouflaged by houses and dusty walls)

(enthroned we covet the park)
this our arena   this our bullfight.

5

Nightly, the castle is bat shrieks.
                                    Illuminated
                (in a scriptorium
                a monk bent double in the dim light
                his numb fingers plume)

in this pool of darkened valley
the castle glimmers from the mountain top.
                                    A torch.

Slender firs enclose its walls
like wheat vulnerable to the scythe
their trunks don't hide   they beckon.

Shall I fortress you
in my arms, you an uncertain ruin.

Notes:

Some of the books befriended or engaged in dialogue...

Breen, David and Kenneth Coates. *The Pacific National Exhibition: An Illustrated History*. University of British Columbia Press: Vancouver, 1982.

Brossard, Nicole. *A Book*. Coach House: Toronto, 1976.

Carr, Angela. *Ropewalk*. Snare Books: Montreal, 2006.

Jabès, Edmond. *Le Livre des Questions*. Gallimard: France, 1991.

Kim, Myung Mi. *Commons*. University of California Press: Berkeley, 2002.

Kogawa, Joy. *Obasan*. Penguin Books: Toronto, 1981.

Kroetsch, Robert. *The Ledger*. Brick Books: London, 1997.

Marlatt, Daphne and Robert Minden. *Steveston*. Ronsdale Press: Vancouver, 2001.

Moure, Erín. *O Cidadán*. House of Anansi Press: Toronto, 2002.

Robertson, Lisa. *Debbie: An Epic*. New Star Books: Vancouver, 1997.

Robertson, Lisa. *Rousseau's Boat*. Nomados: Vancouver, 2004.

Acknowledgements:

Poems from this collection have appeared in *The Capilano Review*, *Event*, *filling Station*, *Matrix* (2004, 2007), *Portfolio Milieu* (Canada), *NO: A Journal for the Arts* (USA), and in two chapbooks: *Close Your Eyes* (with drawings by Anthony Burnham) (Delirium Press, 2005) and *The Dictator's Garden* (Pressdust, 2003).

A visual installation based on "Spirit of the West!" will appear in the exhibition *Less is More: The Poetics of Erasure* at Simon Fraser University Gallery in Vancouver, Nov.1-Dec.12, 2008.

Thank you to the City of Vancouver Archives for the research time under their grass roof and to the Canada Council for the Arts and Sage Hill for their valuable support.

Thank you to Stephanie Bolster for initially fairing me into the park, to Betsy Warland and Nicole Brossard for being invaluable to how I wandered while there, and to Erín Moure for being a park enthusiast and for her close reading, inspiration and companionship in poetries.

Thank you as well to Douglas Barbour for the finishing touches and Noelle Allen at Wolsak and Wynn Publishers whose generous support allows the park to be public.

And thank you to Anthony Burnham for giving the park its own special look, and to Thierry Collins for bringing a part of it into 16 mm.

Oana Avasilichioaei is a poet and translator (French and Romanian). Her first poetry collection *Abandon* (Wolsak and Wynn, 2005) will soon appear in Spanish translation as *Abandono* (Tinta Nueva, Mexico City, 2008). Her translation of Romanian poet Nichita Stănescu titled *Occupational Sickness* was published in 2006 (BuschekBooks). Oana lives in Montreal where she translates and coordinates the Atwater Poetry Project reading series.

Praise for *Abandon* by Oana Avasilichiaoei:

From the mildly menacing first line of "Dragon," the long poem that begins *Abandon*, it is clear that Oana Avasilichioaei's first collection will be no ordinary book of Canadian poetry.
– *The Malahat Review*

Abandon is original in concept and bold and deft in execution.
– *Academia*

These poems capture absence, like smoke after fire, a hoarse whisper from a choked throat.
– *Prairie Fire*